Medieval Tech Today

Do We BUILD Like It's MEDIEVAL Times?

Construction Technology THEN and NOW

by Megan Cooley Peterson

Content Consultant:
Jennifer M. Feltman, PhD
Assistant Professor of Medieval Art and Architecture
Department of Art and Art History
The University of Alabama

CAPSTONE PRESS
a capstone imprint

Captivate is published by Capstone Press, an imprint of Capstone.
1710 Roe Crest Drive
North Mankato, Minnesota 56003
www.capstonepub.com

Library of Congress Cataloging-in-Publication Data is available on the Library of Congress website.
ISBN: 978-1-4966-8472-1 (hardcover)
ISBN: 978-1-4966-8492-9 (eBook PDF)

Summary:
From cranes to castles, medieval innovators helped develop and improve some important construction technology we use today. The Middle Ages were crucial for the development of technologies such as the chimney, central heating, the flying buttress, and more! Discover how we still build like we're in medieval times, with interesting historical facts, scientific details, and illuminating photos.

Image Credits
Alamy: DV TRAVEL, 17, PRISMA ARCHIVO, 33, Walker Art Library, 19, (Top), Zoltán Csipke, 20; Getty Images/Arterra/Contributor, 31, Print Collector/Contributor, 35; Newscom/imageBROKER/FB-Rose, 25, ZUMA Press/Ben Birchall, 16; Shutterstock: andyparker72, 21, Anita van den Broek, 19, (Bottom), Anton_Ivanov, 41, Bill Perry, 13, canadastock, 29, Claudio Divizia, 39, emperorcosar, 43, Faraways, 23, FXQuadro, 11, Hypervision Creative, 27, jianbing Lee, 28, Kiev.Victor, 9, Malgorzata Liitkowska, 26, Mike Mareen, 42-43, Oleg_P, Cover, (Bottom Left), OSTILL is Franck Camhi, 14, Pierdelune, 15, Rastislav Sedlak SK, 4-5, Rita Robinson, Cover, (Bottom Right), sloukam, 6, StockPhotosArt, 37, The Toidi, 34

Design Elements
Capstone; Shutterstock: andromina, Curly Pat, derGriza, Evgeniya Mokeeva, KittyVector, Kompaniets Taras, lightmood, ONYXprj, Tartila, yalcinart

Editorial Credits
Editor: Eliza Leahy; Designer: Sarah Bennett; Media Researcher: Jo Miller; Production Specialist: Katy LaVigne

Printed and bound in the United States of America.
PA117

Table of Contents

Words in **bold** are in the glossary.

CHAPTER 1

Modern or Medieval?

From soaring skyscrapers to jaw-dropping bridges, builders today are always testing the limits. In 2004, architects in Dubai, United Arab Emirates, decided to make history. They wanted to construct the tallest building the world had ever seen. Giant cranes lifted steel and glass high into the sky. After four years of construction, the Burj Khalifa building rose approximately 2,716 feet (828 meters) above the ground. It remains the world's tallest building.

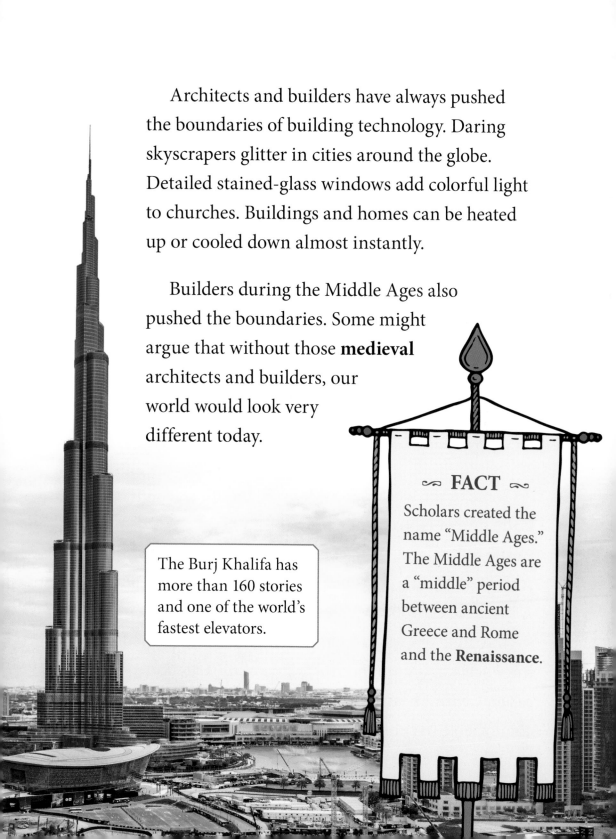

Architects and builders have always pushed the boundaries of building technology. Daring skyscrapers glitter in cities around the globe. Detailed stained-glass windows add colorful light to churches. Buildings and homes can be heated up or cooled down almost instantly.

Builders during the Middle Ages also pushed the boundaries. Some might argue that without those **medieval** architects and builders, our world would look very different today.

The Burj Khalifa has more than 160 stories and one of the world's fastest elevators.

∼ FACT ∼
Scholars created the name "Middle Ages." The Middle Ages are a "middle" period between ancient Greece and Rome and the **Renaissance**.

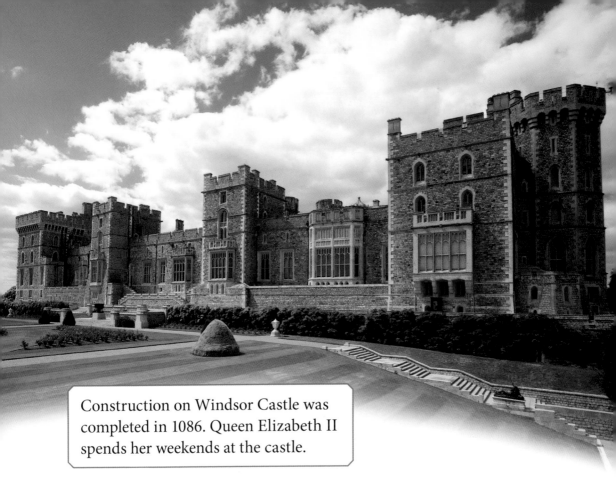

Construction on Windsor Castle was completed in 1086. Queen Elizabeth II spends her weekends at the castle.

Some of the world's most famous buildings, from the Cathedral of Notre Dame in Paris, France, to Windsor Castle in England, were constructed during the Middle Ages. The Middle Ages in Europe lasted from around AD 476 to AD 1500. Medieval builders didn't settle for the same old way of doing things. They developed the wheelbarrow and cranes to make construction easier. Central heating made homes and buildings more comfortable in cold weather. Stained-glass windows brought bold colors to cathedrals and churches.

Today, many homes around the world are built of wood. The same was true during the Middle Ages. Pine forests blanketed northern Europe during that time. Builders used timber to construct houses, churches, and grand estates. Because wood burns easily, most medieval structures have not survived.

The Three Periods of the Middle Ages

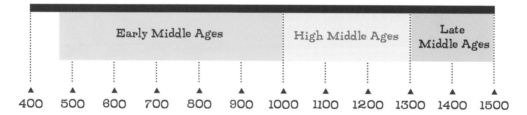

| | | Early Middle Ages | | | | | High Middle Ages | | | Late Middle Ages | |

400 500 600 700 800 900 1000 1100 1200 1300 1400 1500

The Wheelbarrow

Medieval construction improved with the use of the wheelbarrow. Before the wheelbarrow, workers moved heavy materials by hand or with a handbarrow. A handbarrow was similar to a wheelbarrow, only it didn't have a wheel. Today's electric wheelbarrows can carry much heavier loads than a regular wheelbarrow.

CHAPTER 2

Stained Glass

Have you ever been inside a church or building with stained-glass windows? When the sunlight hits these windows, the colorful glass glows. Stained glass can tell a story in pictures, almost like a book can. Glass companies make sheets of colored glass. Artists trace designs onto the glass and cut them out. The pieces are joined by lead or copper foil.

In the Middle Ages, electricity hadn't yet been discovered. People couldn't flick a switch to brighten up a room. They had to use natural sources, such as sunlight and fire. In the Middle Ages, some churches in Europe began installing colorful stained-glass windows. As the sunlight passed through them, the windows cast colorful light into the church.

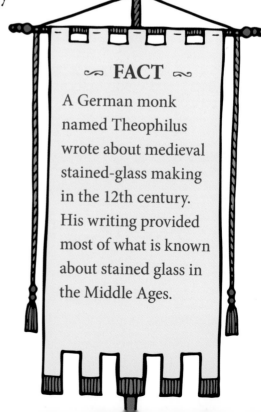

∾ FACT ∾

A German monk named Theophilus wrote about medieval stained-glass making in the 12th century. His writing provided most of what is known about stained glass in the Middle Ages.

Medieval stained-glass windows told stories from the Bible. Since many medieval people couldn't read, it was an easy way to teach them about the Bible. Many churches still have their original stained-glass windows from the Middle Ages. The Cathedral of Chartres in Chartres, France, was constructed in the late 1100s and early 1200s. Its huge stained-glass **lancet** window was made around 1150. A lancet window is a tall, narrow window that has an arch at the top.

The middle window, known as the Incarnation Window, tells the story of Jesus Christ's birth.

Turning Glass into Art

Medieval glassmakers made clear glass out of sand and ashes. The ashes came from burnt seaweed or wood. They heated the sand and ashes until they became **molten** glass. As the glass cooled, it hardened into thin sheets. To make colored glass, glassmakers added **metal oxides** to the sand and ashes. Iron oxide turned the glass green and brown. Manganese gave the glass a purple color. For blue glass, cobalt oxide was added.

Medieval Windows

Can you imagine a house without glass windows? Most homes and buildings in the Middle Ages didn't have them! Glass windows were too expensive. Horn windowpanes were less expensive and more common. Cattle horns were boiled and made into thin sheets. They let in light, but you couldn't see through them.

Today's stained-glass windows are made in much the same way they were in the Middle Ages.

Artists crafted the colored glass into stained-glass windows. First, a glass painter would draw the window's design on a tabletop or sheet of paper. A glass cutter cut out the shapes for the painter, who painted on the designs. The glass had to be heated again so the paint would stick. For the last step, the glass painter put all the pieces of glass back together. Then strips of lead were **soldered** to hold the pieces together.

CHAPTER 3

The Flying Buttress

The Cathedral of Notre Dame in Paris is one of the most famous buildings in the world. Millions of people visit this centuries-old church every year. One of the building's most striking features is its flying buttresses. These external stone arches look almost like a spider's legs. They make the building's walls stronger. Without these arches, the walls would collapse under the weight of the stone ceiling and stained-glass windows.

Visitors to Notre Dame have medieval architects to thank for the flying buttress. Construction began in 1163. Until that time, most buildings were constructed in the Romanesque style. This style had thick walls and round arches to support the building's weight. Heavy walls limited the number of windows the building could carry. This meant Romanesque buildings had very few windows.

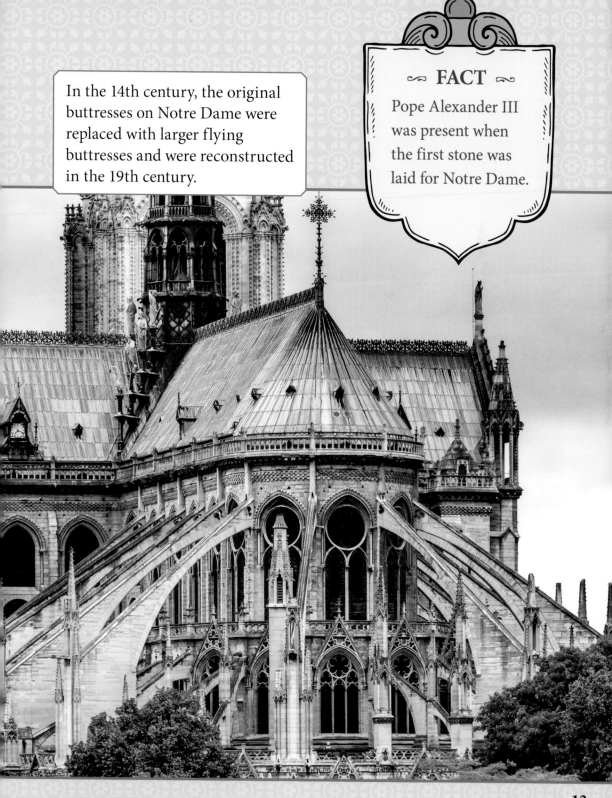

In the 14th century, the original buttresses on Notre Dame were replaced with larger flying buttresses and were reconstructed in the 19th century.

Builders wanted to include many stained-glass windows in their design of Notre Dame. They knew the building would need thin walls. The architects used a relatively new building technique to solve this problem—the flying buttress. Some historians argue that Notre Dame featured the first externally visible flying buttresses.

The flying buttress is an exterior support that uses an arch called a flyer. The arch almost appears to be "flying" from the building into the exterior buttress. Flying buttresses helped the walls support the weight of vaulted ceilings and heavy stained-glass windows. If you look up

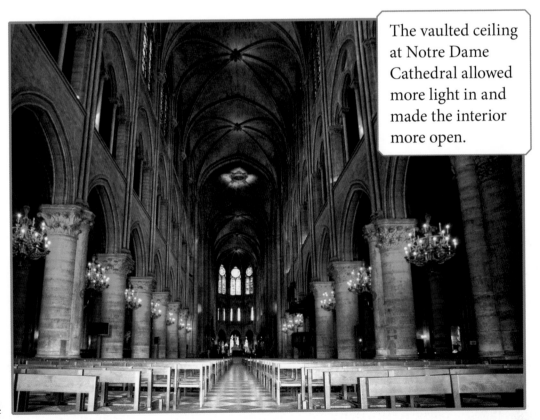

The vaulted ceiling at Notre Dame Cathedral allowed more light in and made the interior more open.

at a vaulted ceiling, it looks like an upside-down boat. Vaulted ceilings meet at a point.

Architects today use the flying buttress in their designs because it looks cool. Modern flying buttresses can be made from stone, steel, or concrete.

Flying buttresses give strength to the Washington National Cathedral in Washington, D.C. Construction on this building lasted from 1907 to 1990.

CHAPTER 4

The Treadwheel Crane

A crane nicknamed "Big Carl" is one of the world's largest. This supersized piece of equipment can lift several thousand tons. The crane needs 12 motors to run it. Workers spent three months putting Big Carl together in southwest England in 2019. They are using it to build a nuclear power plant. The plant should be finished in 2025.

Big Carl's main hook weighs more than 115 tons.

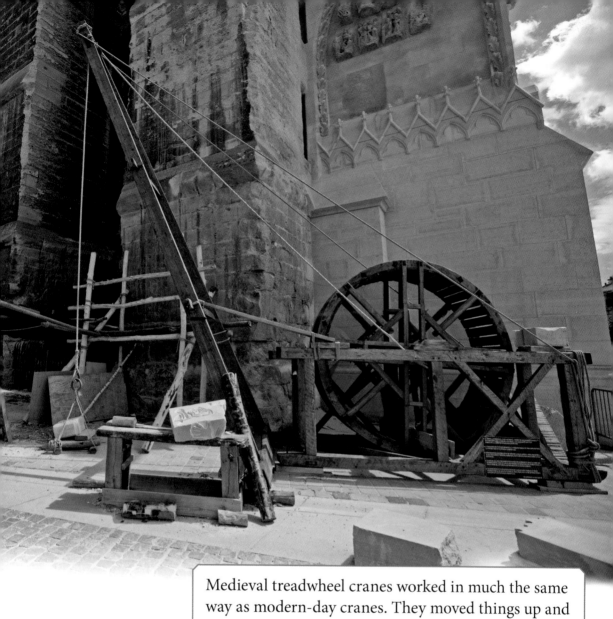

Medieval treadwheel cranes worked in much the same way as modern-day cranes. They moved things up and down by pulley, but without machine power.

Medieval builders also constructed large buildings, from Notre Dame Cathedral to massive stone castles. And they didn't have motorized cranes. They used cranes made from wood! But without engines, how did they do it?

Ancient Roman Cranes

Wooden cranes were used in ancient Rome. Early cranes had a V-shaped **jib**. The jib was made from two pieces of thick wood. A rope passed through a pulley at the top of the jib. A crank at the bottom of the jib raised or lowered the rope. Workers turned the crank by hand. Later, the crank was replaced by a large treadwheel. Men walked inside the wheel to power it.

After the Roman Empire fell, builders forgot about the treadwheel crane. Early medieval buildings were built using smaller stones. The stones had to be light enough for workers to carry and place by hand.

Reinventing the Treadwheel Crane

Carrying stone by hand was hard work. Medieval builders knew there had to be an easier way. They likely turned a windlass into a

⌁ **FACT** ⌁

The first written record of a medieval treadwheel crane came from France in 1225. In England, the first written record of a treadwheel crane came in 1331.

treadwheel crane. A windlass is powered by a hand-turned crank or spoked wheel instead of a treadwheel. Later, planks were added to the wheel. Now men could walk inside the wheel to turn it.

Windlasses and treadwheel cranes were used to lift heavy materials in medieval Europe.

Salisbury Cathedral in England had a windlass installed to help build its spire in the early 1300s. It remains in the church to this day.

Medieval Treadwheel Cranes

Most medieval treadwheel crane wheels were about 16 feet (5 m) across—big enough for two men to fit inside! As the men walked inside the wheel, the crane slowly lifted the object. During construction, treadwheel cranes were probably placed on the ground inside the building. As the building got taller, workers moved the crane to upper levels. The crane could be taken apart and put back together.

⤳ FACT ⤳

It was easier for medieval builders to leave treadwheel cranes inside a building when construction was completed. If future renovations were needed, the crane would be handy.

Mont-Saint-Michel Abbey in France still has its medieval treadwheel crane.

Early medieval treadwheel cranes could only lift and lower objects. They could not move from side to side. Art from the mid-1300s shows some of the first treadwheel cranes that could **pivot**.

After the Middle Ages

Crane technology continued to advance after the Middle Ages ended. In the 1800s, steam-powered iron cranes replaced wooden treadwheel cranes. They were stronger and could lift heavier loads. Men didn't have to walk on these cranes to get them to move. The next time you see a crane building a skyscraper or bridge, remember how far this medieval technology has come.

The Fairbairn steam-powered crane in England was built in 1878.

CHAPTER 5

The Stationary Harbor Crane

Every day, ships travel the oceans delivering goods, food, and materials to almost every country on Earth. Container ships carry truckloads of goods packed into containers. Each container must be carefully stacked on the ship.

Once a container ship arrives at the dock, harbor cranes take over. Mobile harbor cranes can drive around the dock. They lift containers on and off the ships. The world economy wouldn't be what it is today without these ships and the harbor cranes that keep products moving.

Medieval builders had to move materials and goods too. They didn't have modern highways or powerful ships like we do today. After the Roman Empire ended, roads became rutted and filled with holes. New roads weren't built. It was safer and less expensive to move building materials by water.

When you buy something at a store or order it online, chances are it traveled on a container ship and was unloaded by a harbor crane like this one.

Workers wanted ships loaded and unloaded as quickly as possible. The faster the goods were unloaded, the sooner they could be sold or used for construction projects. Before the harbor crane, men carried goods and supplies to and from ships on wooden boards called gangplanks. Imagine trying to carry a heavy load while balancing on a wobbly plank!

Harbor towns were bustling places in the Middle Ages. Buildings and harbor cranes were often constructed right on the water's edge. The harbor crane was invented around the same time as the treadwheel crane but was larger. Harbor cranes had to haul much heavier loads.

Harbor cranes used double treadwheels. These wheels were typically larger than regular treadwheel cranes. A harbor crane's treadwheel could be 21 feet (6.5 m) across. Larger wheels could support more weight, and double wheels made them quicker. Harbor cranes also pivoted. Unlike treadwheel cranes, harbor cranes were permanent structures.

Medieval harbor cranes like this one in Lüneburg, Germany, had roofs to keep the machinery and workers dry.

CHAPTER 6

The Segmental Arch Bridge

In Fayetteville, West Virginia, the New River Gorge Bridge spans 3,030 feet (924 m). It soars 876 feet (267 m) above roaring waters. The bridge's segmental arch is 1,700 feet (518 m) wide. Construction was completed in 1977. It remained the world's longest single-span arch bridge until 2003. The Chaotianmen Bridge in China now holds the record at 5,712 feet (1,741 m) long.

The New River Gorge Bridge is the longest steel arch bridge in the United States. It weighs an impressive 44,000 tons.

The Sydney Harbour Bridge is 3,770 feet (1,149 m) long.

Arch bridges are among the most famous bridges in the world. The Sydney Harbour Bridge is a steel arch bridge in Sydney, Australia. Opened in 1932, the bridge has four railroad tracks and a highway. People can walk across this famous bridge.

The arch bridge is also one of the oldest types of bridges. These bridges have been constructed since ancient times. In the Middle Ages, goods needed to be moved quickly and easily over rivers. In crowded cities, some bridges even became building sites! Homes, shops, and churches were built on top of bridges.

The Great Stone Bridge is also known as the Anji Bridge and the Zhaozhou Bridge.

The First Segmental Arch Bridge

Chinese architect Li Chun designed one of the world's first segmental arch bridges in the early 600s. His Great Stone Bridge is still used today. The segmental arch is a segment of a circle instead of a half circle. Segmental arches are stronger and lighter than semicircle arch bridges. They also use fewer materials, allowing water to flow under them more easily.

Medieval Segmental Arch Bridges

Medieval bridge builders started constructing segmental arch bridges in the later Middle Ages. The Pont Saint-Bénézet in Avignon, France, was completed in 1185. The bridge had 22 segmental arches and was about 3,000 feet (914 m) long. The bridge even had a chapel! Most of the bridge was destroyed in 1226 during a siege of the city.

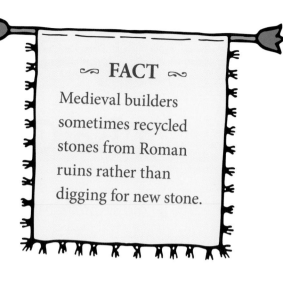

Medieval bridges were also built as a form of defense. In the early Middle Ages, the Vikings often invaded French cities. They would sail up the Seine and other major rivers to **raid** inland cities. Finally, French kings had bridges built along the rivers to stop the Vikings. The Vikings' ships couldn't get past the bridges.

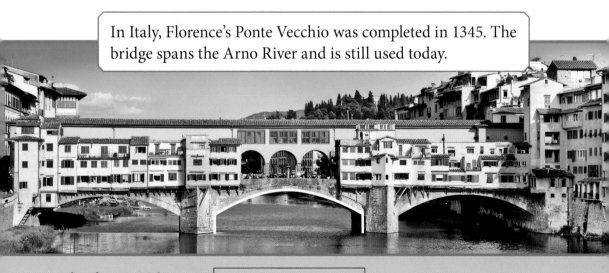

In Italy, Florence's Ponte Vecchio was completed in 1345. The bridge spans the Arno River and is still used today.

central arch span 86 feet

rise of 11 feet, 6 inches

CHAPTER 7

The Chimney

It's a cold winter's night, and you're curled up in front of the fireplace. The flames crackle and dance, warming the room. Smoke from neighboring chimneys puffs into the night sky.

Many homes and buildings around the world use fireplaces. Fireplaces burn wood or are run by gas. Chimneys easily vent smoke and gases outside, keeping rooms smoke-free. Chimneys can be made of brick or steel. But have you ever wondered about where and when the chimney was invented?

Staying warm during the Middle Ages wasn't easy. Medieval people didn't have modern furnaces or electric heat. Finding ways to keep out the cold would have been a constant worry. During the early Middle Ages, people dug pits in the center of a room. They built a fire in the pit and used it to cook food. The fire also heated the room. Later, hearths replaced open pits. A hearth is a stone or brick platform where a fire burns. Smoke rose up through a small hole or

Medieval homes were not well insulated. Hearths like this one in a Belgian shipowner's home were important for keeping warm.

vent in the roof. But a lot of it stayed behind, making medieval buildings very smoky places. Smoke hoods also helped clear the room of smoke. The hoods were placed directly over the fire. Smoke went up the hood and out through the roof.

In stone buildings, hearths were sometimes placed along the walls. Since stones can't burn, there was no fear of setting the walls on fire. The smoke hoods were attached to the walls. By the end of the 12th century, builders added **flues** inside the stone walls. The flues were attached to the hoods. Smoke left the building through the flue.

The Medieval Chimney

By the late 1200s, builders moved the flue. They ran it along the exterior wall, and it developed into a chimney. Soon, chimneys were also added to wooden buildings. Builders coated the inside of wooden chimneys with plaster to keep them from catching fire. The hearths were made of stone, tile, or brick. As medieval workers created the chimney, they began placing the hearth deeper into the exterior wall. Soon, the hearths looked like fireplaces of today.

Improving the Chimney

The medieval chimney likely influenced modern ventilation systems. Today's kitchen vent hoods look much like smoke hoods used in the Middle Ages.

Like chimneys, modern air exchangers push stale air outside our homes. But they also pull fresh outside air in.

Before the chimney was invented, smoke was directed out of buildings through a flue.

CHAPTER 8

Central Heating

Central heating is one of the most popular ways to heat a home or building today. A central heating unit starts at a boiler or furnace. A boiler heats water to very high temperatures. Then a pump pushes the heated water through pipes around the building. Heat **radiates** from the pipes to warm the rooms. A furnace burns natural gas to heat the air. The hot air is then forced through ducts around the building. The warm air enters a room through a vent.

Medieval people enjoyed the comforts of central heating too. In fact, they improved upon other heating systems. But their system was not as easy to operate as central heating today.

Central heating is controlled by a **thermostat**. You just choose a temperature and let the system do the work.

The Roman Hypocaust

Medieval builders took a heating system called the hypocaust and made it better. The hypocaust was used during the Roman Empire. Builders placed a hypocaust underneath a room on ground level. A fire burning in the hypocaust's furnace heated the floor above. The heated floor radiated heat into the room.

Smaller versions of the hypocaust were built in the Middle Ages. They were less expensive and burned cheaper materials, such as twigs and hay. In the frigid winters, hypocausts had to be fired almost constantly. As soon as the hypocaust's fire went out, the heat vanished.

wall flue carrying hot gases to upper floor

stoke hole

tiles

tiles

mosaic floor

concrete

square piers

concrete

Hypocausts were first used during the Roman Empire to heat buildings.

35

Heat Storage Hypocaust

Medieval builders came up with a heat storage hypocaust around the early 1300s. They piled granite stones on top of the hypocaust's furnace. The stones absorbed the fire's heat. Builders also placed a hot plate in the floor directly above the furnace. Holes in the hot plate could be opened or closed.

To use the heat storage hypocaust, a fire was lit in the furnace. The holes in the hot plate were kept closed. As the fire burned, it heated up the stones. Smoke vented out through a chimney in the wall. After the fire was put out, the holes in the hot plate were opened, letting heat out. After just one fire, the stones released heat for days. The heat storage hypocaust was much more efficient than open hearths and fireplaces. Central heating was here to stay.

The Malbork Castle Experiment

Malbork Castle in Poland had a heat storage hypocaust installed below its banquet hall in the 1400s. In 1822, castle staff decided to test the 400-year-old hypocaust. They lit a fire for three and a half hours. Then they opened the air vents. The air temperature rose from 43 to 72 degrees Fahrenheit (6 to 23 Celsius) in 20 minutes. Six days after the fire was put out, the stones were still releasing warm air.

Hypocausts were used to heat public bathhouses in ancient Rome.

CHAPTER 9

Gothic Architecture

Gothic Revival architecture became popular in England and the United States in the 1700s and 1800s. Many buildings and private homes were built in this style. Construction on England's Westminster Palace lasted from 1840 to 1860. The country's government is housed there. Private homes built in this style often had pointed windows and castle-like towers. Gothic homes can still be found in many neighborhoods today.

A Modern Medieval Castle

Medieval castle construction continues to fascinate builders today. In 1997, expert builders gathered in Treigny, France, to build a castle using only medieval building technology. The building site for Guédelon Castle is located near a quarry and forest, giving workers access to natural building materials. Treadwheel cranes and horse-drawn carts are used to move materials. The building will be finished in 2023.

A.W. Pugin helped design Westminster as well as the palace's famous Big Ben clock tower. These revival buildings had pointed windows, stained glass, and spires.

This popular style was developed during the Middle Ages. The Gothic castle and cathedral are the most famous kinds of medieval architecture. Movies and TV shows about the Middle Ages show royalty living in stone castles. But to pull off these massive builds, medieval workers had to try new ways of building.

Before the Middle Ages, Roman buildings had thick walls and round arches. Over time, masons had the idea to try pointed arches, which turned out to be stronger than round ones. Medieval European architects likely borrowed pointed arches from earlier styles of architecture in Spain.

Medieval builders wanted their churches to reach high into the sky. Flying buttresses strengthened the buildings, allowing them to reach great heights. Because the buttresses are placed outside of Gothic buildings, they make the interior space seem even more grand.

The Basilica of Saint-Denis just outside of Paris is considered one of the first true Gothic buildings. The church was originally built in the 600s. By the 1100s, it needed to be enlarged. Builders used pointed arches, segmented rib vaults, and exterior buttresses to expand the church.

Stained-glass windows throughout the Basilica of Saint-Denis let in colored light.

Castles

In the Middle Ages, kings and lords lived in castles, along with their servants. Early medieval castles were usually small and built of wood. A wooden fence surrounded an open space, and a wooden tower sat on a hill. These simple castles couldn't withstand attacks, and they burned down easily. By the 12th century, castle builders used stone or brick instead of wood. Attackers couldn't easily break through a stone wall.

Medieval Construction Technology Today

The Middle Ages ended more than 500 years ago. But the influence of medieval construction technology can still be seen today. From soaring tower cranes to cozy fireplace chimneys, medieval construction technology didn't stay stuck in the Middle Ages.

Dracula's Castle?

Bran Castle in Romania may have inspired the Irish novelist Bram Stoker. Some readers say Stoker based the fictional castle in his 1897 novel *Dracula* on Bran Castle. But Stoker never stepped foot inside the castle. He may have only read about it.

Construction on Bran Castle took place from 1377 to 1388.

Malbork Castle is one of the most famous Gothic-style castles. Built in the late 12th century, it's the world's largest brick Gothic castle.

Timeline of Technology

500s
Churches in Europe begin installing stained-glass windows.

Early 1200s
Use of the wheelbarrow becomes widespread in Europe.

1225
The earliest documentation of a medieval treadwheel crane in France is written; the harbor crane is also developed around this time.

605
Chinese architect Li Chun designs one of the world's first segmental arch bridges.

Late 1200s
The chimney is developed in Europe.

Early 1100s
Gothic architecture is developed in Europe. This style is defined by thin walls, tall towers, flying buttresses, and stained-glass windows.

1163 to 1250
The Cathedral of Notre Dame is constructed in a new Gothic style in Paris.

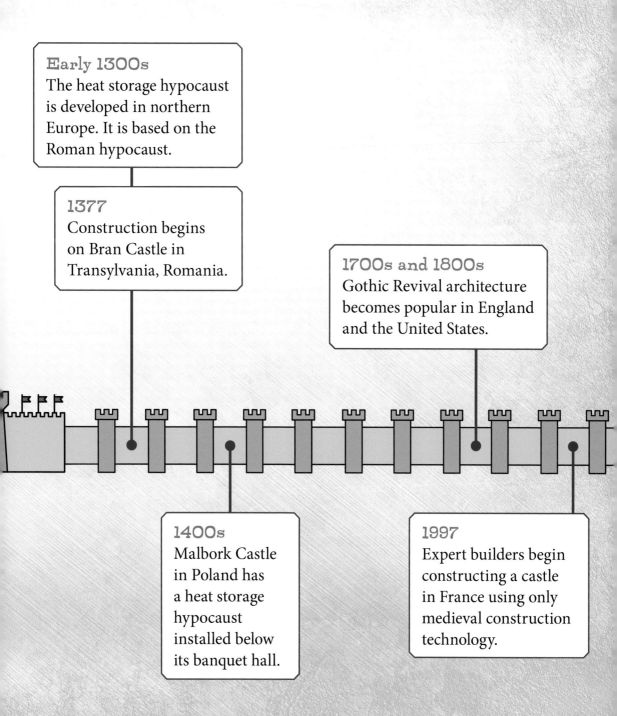

Early 1300s
The heat storage hypocaust is developed in northern Europe. It is based on the Roman hypocaust.

1377
Construction begins on Bran Castle in Transylvania, Romania.

1700s and 1800s
Gothic Revival architecture becomes popular in England and the United States.

1400s
Malbork Castle in Poland has a heat storage hypocaust installed below its banquet hall.

1997
Expert builders begin constructing a castle in France using only medieval construction technology.

Glossary

flue (FLU)—a channel through which smoke can escape

jib (JIB)—the arm of a crane that lifts loads

lancet (LAN-sit)—a tall, narrow window that has an arch at the top

medieval (mee-DEE-vuhl)—having to do with the period of history between AD 476 and 1500

metal oxide (MET-uhl OKS-ide)—a chemical compound formed between metals and oxygen

molten (MOHLT-uhn)—melted by heat into a liquid; molten glass can be poured into molds

pivot (PIV-uht)—to turn or balance on a point

radiate (RAY-dee-ate)—to give off energy

raid (RAYD)—a sudden surprise attack on a place

Renaissance (REN-uh-sahnss)—a period in Europe beginning in the 14th century and ending in the mid-17th century that is noted for its cultural achievements

solder (SAHD-uhr)—to join pieces of glass by putting a small amount of heated, melted alloy between them; as the alloy cools, it hardens

thermostat (THUR-muh-stat)—a device that controls the temperature of the air in heating and cooling systems

Read More

Lim, Annalees. *Once Upon a Medieval Craft.* Minneapolis: Lerner Publications, 2018.

Sebastian, Emily, ed. *Technology of the Medieval and Early Modern Worlds.* New York: Britannica Educational Publishing, in association with Rosen Educational Services, 2016.

Steele, Philip. *Castles.* London: Dorling Kindersley Limited, 2019.

Internet Sites

DK Find Out! Castles
https://www.dkfindout.com/us/history/castles/

Guédelon Castle
https://www.guedelon.fr/en/

Select Bibliography

Clark, William W. "The First Flying Buttresses: A New Reconstruction of the Nave of Notre-Dame de Paris." *The Art Bulletin* Vol. 66, No. 1 (March, 1984), pp. 47–65.

Dresbeck, LeRoy. "The Chimney and Social Change in Medieval England." *Albion: A Quarterly Journal Concerned with British Studies.* Vol. 3, No. 1 (Spring, 1971), pp. 21–32.

Newman, Paul B. *Daily Life in the Middle Ages.* London: McFarland & Co., 2001.

Index